Sebastian Gardner

I Lost My Virginity to Chopin's Nocturne in B-Flat Minor

Produced by Paper Mug Theatre

Salamander Street

PLAYS

First published in 2021 by Salamander Street Ltd.
(info@salamanderstreet.com)

I Lost My Virginity to Chopin's Nocturne in B-Flat Minor © Sebastian Gardner, 2021

All rights reserved.

Application for professional and amateur performance rights should be directed to the author c/o Salamander Street. No performance may be given unless a licence has been obtained, and no alterations may be made in the title or the text of the adaptation without the author's prior written consent.

You may not copy, store, distribute, transmit, reproduce or otherwise make available this publication (or any part of it) in any form, or binding or by any means (print, electronic, digital, optical, mechanical, photocopying, recording or otherwise), without the prior written permission of the publisher. Any person who does any unauthorized act in relation to this publication may be liable to criminal prosecution and civil claims for damages.

ISBN: 9781914228162

10 9 8 7 6 5 4 3 2 1

For Nichola and Robin.

Acknowledgements

I Lost My Virginity to Chopin's Nocturne in B-Flat Minor premiered at The Vaults Theatre, London, on 21st August 2021.

Produced by Paper Mug Theatre.

With special thanks to Uri Roodner, Christopher Brett Bailey, Rory Thomas-Howes, Lily Sinko, Josh Tucker and Katie Galbraith.

Characters

OLLIE

LAURA

CAST LIST

OLLIE   *Sebastian Gardner*

LAURA   *Anouche-Alana Chokarian*

CREATIVE TEAM

DIRECTOR   *Ami Okumura Jones*

PRODUCER   *Sam Edmunds*

STAGE MANAGER   *Louise Oliver*

DESIGNER   *Blythe Brett*

ARTWORK   *Estée Angéline Alleno-Powell*

This play takes place in a real room, and in real time – but stage directions are indicative, and not prescriptive, and should be determined by the context.

A forward slash mark (/) marks the point of interruption in overlapping dialogue.

There is no interval.

Act One

Late winter, 2019.

The living room of an open-plan flat in Shoreditch, East London. It's lived in, but not untidy.

On the coffee table, in the centre of the room, there is a large bouquet of balloons.

A number of them have the same picture of a man's face on, with a large, transparent balloon filled with confetti, floating above the rest, with the words 'Will You Marry Me?' in large gold letters.

Suddenly **OLLIE**, *26, bursts through the front door. He clambers into the living room, stumbling over a full shoe rack in his path. He grabs hold of the bouquet of balloons and begins to search for a place to hide them. His search becomes more and more frantic the longer it goes on.*

Finally, he spots a large ottoman in the corner of the room. He kicks off the lid, and with one hand firmly on the bouquet, begins to empty the contents of the ottoman, sending blankets and various jumpers flying across the flat. Once it's empty, he starts stuffing the balloons into the ottoman.

Just as he reaches for the lid, **LAURA**, *24, bursts through the open door.*

LAURA: Don't you fucking run away from me you impotent little shit.

 OLLIE *slams the lid shut.*

OLLIE: Laura –

LAURA: Self-righteous,

OLLIE: Laur –

LAURA: – arrogant, pathetic –

 LAURA *clocks the shoe rack, shoes and various blankets that are strewn across the flat.*

LAURA: What the fuck is this?

OLLIE: *(Struggling to find an answer.)* I'm… wound up!

LAURA: *You're wound up?*

OLLIE: I kicked it in a fit of rage.

LAURA: Oh I'm sorry, I didn't realise that all these years I've been fucking my teenage son.

OLLIE: Laura can/ you please try to keep your voice –

LAURA: If you dare tell me to keep my fucking voice down, I swear I will tear out your throat with my bare hands.

Silence.

OLLIE: You're clearly feeling very worked up…

LAURA: Fuck you.

OLLIE: But we're not going to get anywhere when you're in this state, so just take a moment to –

LAURA *grabs a glass off the coffee table.*

LAURA: Tell me to calm down, see what happens.

OLLIE *stands motionless, as does* **LAURA**. *They have a brief stand-off.*

OLLIE *goes to speak,* **LAURA** *raises the glass behind her,* **OLLIE** *stops himself.*

LAURA *slams the glass back down.*

OLLIE: *(Under his breath.)* Christ, you're tapped.

LAURA *turns and launches the glass towards* **OLLIE**, *narrowly missing his head. It shatters as it meets the wall.*

Silence.

LAURA: You just couldn't drop it.

OLLIE: It was/ his to drop –

LAURA: There were so many opportunities for you to change the subject and move on, but you couldn't even do that.

OLLIE: Because he wasn't *hearing* what I was *saying*.

LAURA: Everyone heard what you were saying; the people in the pub next door heard what you were saying.

OLLIE: Don't exaggerate –

LAURA: You went on and on for hours –

OLLIE: Because he needed me to explain my point –

LAURA: Because you love it.

OLLIE: Love what?

LAURA: I've seen you argue with people about things you don't even give a shit about. It's not impressive. It's boring. You don't realise that the things you say affect people.

OLLIE: I'm a very effective converser –

LAURA: Yes, but you don't have to engage with –

OLLIE: Phil said –

LAURA: Don't call him Phil.

OLLIE: Your dad literally said *'the young people who went to the protest didn't have the mental capacity to articulate why they were there'*. If I just smile and nod along, that proves his point.

LAURA: You didn't have to lecture him/ for the best part of an hour like you were overcompensating –

OLLIE: Well quite frankly, I felt he was looking down on me because he's voted in more elections than I have; so maybe I was overcompensating, but I'm sure he couldn't hear me over his overwhelmingly loud ignorance.

Silence.

OLLIE: That was...

I would never intentionally try to embarrass your dad. I engage in conversations about politics with my dad all the time.

LAURA: But you never talk down to him in the way you do to mine.

OLLIE: Potentially because my dad backs up his points with understanding...

LAURA *reacts,* **OLLIE** *instantly tries to backtrack.*

OLLIE: Understanding…. that, research and the sharing of… information… look, my dad –

LAURA: Fuck your dad.

OLLIE: Oh that's lovely.

LAURA: My parents have only met you a handful of times over the last four years. In that time, you have changed. A lot.

OLLIE: I haven't changed –

LAURA: You seem to care an awful lot more about certain things you didn't give a shit about before.

OLLIE: It's called growth.

LAURA: And he probably sees it as flakiness.

OLLIE: I'm open to change. I'm actually listening to what he says when he speaks which is more than I can say for him.

LAURA: He is open to change…

OLLIE: Voting Tory for the first time in your fifties to make sure 'Brexit gets done' doesn't make you open to change. It makes you a…

Fool.

LAURA: A fool?

OLLIE: Yes. A fool. And did I not say, before we left, that your dad tends to play up when he's in front of a group?

LAURA: Well yes, but he –

OLLIE: Thank you. I did see this coming.

LAURA: Well of course *you* saw it coming.

OLLIE: What do you –

LAURA: From the second we walked in you were waiting for a chance to pick a fight with him.

OLLIE: Why would/ I do that?

LAURA: Because you're a cynical little boy who only sees the worst in people.

OLLIE: I am not cynical.

LAURA *gives him a look.*

OLLIE: I'm not!

LAURA: You've been a TA for under a year, and last week you said, *'the younger generation needs a wakeup call'.*

OLLIE: Yea, one of the fucktards spat at me. Spat in my mouth.

LAURA: You probably said something conceited to deserve it.

OLLIE: No actually, because working with SEN kids actually takes a certain level of sensitivity.

LAURA: You just called one of them a fucktard –

OLLIE: Maya's not on the spectrum, she's just dyslexic.

LAURA: Do you only let the non-autistic kids spit in your mouth? Not sure if they told you at work but you can't catch autism.

OLLIE: If you're going to be like this then I'm off out.

LAURA: Ollie, don't go.

OLLIE: Why should I stay? When you belittle –

LAURA: Because I'm pregnant.

Silence.

OLLIE: Are you really?

LAURA: No.

Silence.

OLLIE: Can you even begin to comprehend the level of emotional damage that –

LAURA: Not nearly enough to make us even.

Silence.

LAURA *smirks.*

OLLIE: What was that?

LAURA: What?

OLLIE: You just said something.

LAURA: No I didn't.

OLLIE: Yes you did you went…

He exaggerates her smirk. **LAURA** *laughs.*

LAURA: That was nothing.

OLLIE: Why are you laughing?

LAURA: I'm just laughing. I'm allowed to laugh, or is there a rule/ against laughing?

OLLIE: Don't be like that.

LAURA: Like what?

OLLIE: You're intentionally winding me up.

LAURA: Babe –

OLLIE: Don't babe me. I'm not a babe.

LAURA: Sweet –

OLLIE: Sweetheart is equally patronising.

Silence.

LAURA: I can't believe how upset you get over a fight that you've started.

OLLIE: How on earth did I –

LAURA: Seriously? So just to be clear, you're totally unaware that you were being a cunt?

OLLIE: Please don't use that word.

LAURA: When your girlfriend's parents take you out for dinner –

OLLIE: Lunch.

LAURA: It's not polite to complain about their choice of restaurant.

OLLIE: Firstly, that hole, was not a restaurant. And I didn't complain, your dad asked if anybody had a problem with going to the Montagu Pyke.

LAURA: He was being rhetorical.

OLLIE: Well, I thought he was being genuine. And yes, as it happens, I have a problem with Wetherspoons.

LAURA: How could you possibly –

OLLIE: Excuse me if I refuse to compromise my values and dine in a place that represents everything that is wrong with peak capitalism.

LAURA: Yes, Wetherspoons is evil and I hope Tim Martin dies as soon as possible, but is that really more important than your relationship with my parents?

OLLIE: I just don't want to drink somewhere I don't feel comfortable.

LAURA: You think I feel comfortable at your mum's 'summer soirées' / in aid of finally stopping malaria?

OLLIE: We're not talking about… you're just embarrassed because while everyone else was dressed up –

LAURA: No one over the age of nine has a dress code for a party at their house.

OLLIE: I told you not to wear trainers, but you went and did it anyway, so you only have yourself to blame.

LAURA: I'm sorry to have let down your mum's expectations of the princess you were meant to end up with.

LAURA *starts to roll herself a cigarette.*

OLLIE: My mum likes you an adequate amount, and while you were in a mood the whole day, I had a really nice time.

LAURA: You don't have to defend your mum's party, you can admit it was a bit shit.

OLLIE: She never said it was a party, she said it was an afternoon of fun conversation.

LAURA: Christ, your mum wouldn't know fun if it sat on her face.

Silence.

LAURA *lights her cigarette.*

OLLIE: You could have stayed with your parents tonight, I would have been perfectly happy –

Laura, you don't smoke in here. Go outside.

Silence. **LAURA** *continues to smoke.*

OLLIE *heads over to the cabinet, searches through the top drawer and pulls out a pack of straights. From it, he pulls out a lighter and a cigarette. He lights the cigarette and sits across from* **LAURA**.

Silence.

LAURA *watches* **OLLIE** *with bemusement as he avoids her eyes. After a while, he grabs a nearby mug to flick the ash into.*

Silence.

LAURA: You look pathetic when you try to smoke.

OLLIE *bolts up, puts the cigarette out in the mug and slams it onto the cabinet.*

LAURA: Oh babe, calm down I was –

OLLIE: If you ash on my sofa one more time I won't let you sit there.

OLLIE *heads out to the bedroom.* **LAURA** *takes one last drag of her cigarette before putting it out into the arm of the sofa. She places a coaster over the burn mark, just as* **OLLIE** *returns with a small wooden box. As* **LAURA** *watches him, he pulls out a bag of ketamine and a credit card.*

LAURA: You're joking.

OLLIE: Could *not* be more serious

LAURA: You're such a child.

OLLIE: I don't think a child would be able to purchase elephant ket.

LAURA: What?

OLLIE: What?

LAURA: What in Christ's name is elephant ket?

OLLIE: It's ket, but like, for elephants.

LAURA: There is no such thing.

OLLIE: Well, Max had two lines the other week and he couldn't move for three days.

LAURA: Max did not k-hole from elephant tranquilizer, he just took a lot of ket.

OLLIE: A lot of *elephant* ket.

LAURA: Do you seriously believe there's a different kind of ket for each animal?

OLLIE: They're not gonna use horse tranquilizer on an elephant, it's too big, but I'm sorry if your mum and dad didn't take the time to explain the difference when –

> **LAURA** *blows away* **OLLIE'S** *line of ketamine.*

> **OLLIE** *is speechless.* **LAURA** *moves to the Nespresso machine as they remain in silence.*

OLLIE: I despise you.

LAURA: Really? That's weird, because when I look at you, I feel nothing.

OLLIE: Do you have any idea how few drug dealers actually sell –

> What are you doing?

LAURA: What?

OLLIE: Are you seriously making a coffee in the middle of a tiff?

LAURA: Tiff?

OLLIE: Don't change the subject.

LAURA: No one has ever won an argument by calling it a 'tiff'.

OLLIE: Changed the subject, but ok, why am not allowed to say 'tiff'?

LAURA: Just makes you sound –

OLLIE: What?

LAURA: Like…

OLLIE: Were you going to say gay?

LAURA: Jesus no, It's/ 2019 –

OLLIE: Oh right, so it's okay for you to tell me to 'man-up', but homophobia's off the table?

LAURA: You have got to stop using the 'toxic masculinity card' –

OLLIE: It's not a card, it's a disease that ends lives.

LAURA: We aren't talking about/ toxic masculinity –

OLLIE: Toxic masculinity is the root of the majority of/ mental health issues for young men that lead to depression and suicide –

LAURA: Mental health issues that lead to depression and suicide…

OLLIE: And suicide is the single biggest killer of men under forty-five in the UK.

I am at risk.

LAURA: You do realise that sitting at home and playing COD all day, not very well, is not toxic masculinity, it just makes you a bitch.

OLLIE: Calls herself a feminist, uses words like bitch.

LAURA: You don't always have to have the last word you know, it is possible to just not speak.

OLLIE: I get you –

LAURA: Do ya?

OLLIE: Yep.

LAURA: Good.

OLLIE: Cool.

LAURA: You done?

OLLIE: Uhuh.

LAURA: Fan –

OLLIE: –tastic.

Silence.

> **LAURA** *exits to the kitchen. She returns with a carton of orange juice. She removes the lid and takes a large glug.*

OLLIE: I honestly don't understand why you never use a glass.

LAURA: I honestly don't understand what you get out of being such a self-entitled arsehole.

OLLIE: Entitled? In what way am I entitled?

LAURA: You've always been entitled, you've just never noticed it before, because your nanny never told you.

OLLIE: I never had a nanny.

LAURA: When you were little, who picked you up from primary school?

OLLIE: Not a nanny.

LAURA: Was it your mum?

OLLIE: No, it was her friend, Carol.

LAURA: Why did Carol pick you up, why not your mum?

OLLIE: Because Mum had work, and half the time Carol was going that way, because she cleaned on Tuesdays and –

This is irrelevant, so what if I came from privilege? I don't hide it, I don't deny where I come from. You don't know how conflicting and depressing it feels, you were born working-class. Yes, I was born into money, but I am not entitled.

LAURA: Fine, you're not entitled.

OLLIE: Thank you.

LAURA: Privileged, conceited, inherently deserving, sure. But you're definitely not entitled.

OLLIE: I'm inherently deserving?

LAURA: Oh good, you agree.

OLLIE: Coming from the girl that won't take no for an answer.

LAURA: What the fuck –

OLLIE: Well whenever you initiate and I'm not in the mood –

LAURA: 'Initiate'?

OLLIE: I'm just saying –

LAURA: What exactly are you saying?

OLLIE: Bit rapey.

LAURA: You fucking wish –

OLLIE: Are you implying I long to be raped?

LAURA: Trust the middle-class white boy/ to crowbar in a joke about rape culture.

OLLIE: The fact that I am white… I would never joke about rape culture –

LAURA: Denying it altogether is even more frightening.

OLLIE: You've misinterpreted what I've said.

LAURA: Hey, don't blame me for not understanding your fancy long words, you see, I was born working-class, my school only had one canteen and my mummy didn't pay for my education.

OLLIE: Your mum barely paid you attention, let alone paid for tuition.

LAURA: What did you just say?

OLLIE: Tell me when you're done being spiteful, I'm having a shower.

OLLIE exits to the bedroom. LAURA is left alone.

OLLIE *re-enters with a jumper over his head.*

OLLIE: *(Speaking in a thick accent, intended to be German, and using the arms of the jumper to communicate.)* LAURA!

LAURA: Don't.

OLLIE: I CAN'T HELP BUT NOTICE THAT YOU ARE UPSET.

LAURA: Ollie –

OLLIE: AND I HAVE JUST SEEN OLIVIER, AND HE IS BESIDE HIMSELF.

LAURA: *(Exasperated laugh.)* I fucking hate you

OLLIE *pulls the jumper on and returns to himself.*

OLLIE: And I like you as a friend.

Silence. They both sense the ceasefire.

OLLIE: What are you thinking?

LAURA: I'm thinking… how exhausting it is to have settled. I thought it'd be the easy option, you know? But it turns out it's actually quite a lot of effort.

OLLIE: See, I would be insulted, but at least I achieved something. I overcame an obstacle. I bridged the gap between our market values.

LAURA: You're happy punching?

OLLIE: Of course. You want to die punching. Imagine dying a settler… you'd feel like a failure.

LAURA: You not think you'd be happier if you'd settled then?

OLLIE: I dunno, maybe. But I'm not gonna gamble the happiness I have with you for a chance at happiness with someone else – what's the point?

Silence.

OLLIE: I'm sorry I upset you.

LAURA: I'm not upset that you upset me.

Silence.

OLLIE: I'm sorry I ruined today.

LAURA: You didn't *ruin* –

OLLIE: Can I... please?

It's not like I didn't realise you'd be upset. But the whole thing just escalated so... and I genuinely didn't mean to go all out... but I just felt... slightly... belittled. And even then, I overreacted, and it's not because of your dad, or what he said, I guess... I dunno...

I guess I wasn't feeling myself before we left. If I'm honest, I just needed a day to myself. With you there too, but like, just us. I mean if it was just your parents, then I probably would've coped okay, but then your nan came and suddenly it was a whole big group... social... thing, I mean it was great seeing her but I didn't feel like socialising and, I mean, I don't love seeing people at the best of times, but that's... look, I know that I need to get better at putting on a happy face when we're out –

LAURA: I don't want you to put anything on. I want you to actually be happy when we're out, I don't want you to feel like it's work.

OLLIE: I want to as well, but it's not something you can just switch on and off –

LAURA: Oh Ol... I just think –

OLLIE: What?

LAURA: I don't know... sometimes I think you... and don't, please don't take this... I'm not saying your feelings are irrelevant. But... sometimes I think it all blends into one.

OLLIE: Blends into what?

LAURA: You not *feeling* like yourself with the *effort* of seeing your girlfriend's parents. The need to avoid social events with just... a lack of motivation to do something you can't be bothered to do. You want me to listen and be understanding of how you feel. I am doing my best. But I need the same from you. I need you to stop pretending I'm totally unaffected/ and I am not making this about me. I am looking out for us. If we're gonna have longevity I need you to do that for me./

OLLIE *goes to interject but* **LAURA** *isn't finished.*

Silence.

OLLIE: You said longevity.

LAURA: I did.

OLLIE: You want longevity with me?

LAURA: Yes, I do.

OLLIE *smiles.*

LAURA: What?

OLLIE: I've just never heard you say 'longevity' before.

LAURA: Piss off.

OLLIE: No, I don't mean it in that way, what I mean is, I want longevity with you too. Because I –

LAURA'S *phone rings.*

LAURA: Oh, it's Mum.

LAURA *picks up her baccy and heads out the front.*

OLLIE: Give Phil my love.

LAURA: Fuck you.

Hey Mum. Yea I'm just at home now…

OLLIE *watches her leave. He sits for a bit, gets out his phone and starts scrolling. Suddenly, he remembers the balloons. He shoots up and heads for the ottoman. He checks back at the door before lifting the lid and taking out the balloons.*

He heads for the bedroom, but before he gets there, **LAURA** *re-enters, still on the phone.* **OLLIE** *bolts back into the living room with the balloons. He goes for the ottoman, before realising it's in sight of the hallway. He is flustered, looking around for a place to hide them.* **LAURA** *wonders into the bedroom, still deep in conversation.* **OLLIE** *settles on hiding them behind the sofa, but as he reaches it, another arrangement floats* *up. Becoming more panicked by the second,* **OLLIE** *grabs the second arrangement and heads back to the ottoman, stuffing all the balloons inside. One pops as he tries to close the lid.*

OLLIE: Fuck!

LAURA: *(From the bedroom.)* What?

OLLIE *struggles to close the ottoman.*

OLLIE: I said fuck... the... police...

OLLIE *finally shuts the ottoman just as* **LAURA** *re-enters.*

OLLIE: Who was that?

LAURA: I told you, it was Mum.

OLLIE: Oh, right.

LAURA: She was just checking we got home alright.

OLLIE: Right, yea...

LAURA: This whole thing with her new boss is really getting to her.

OLLIE: Oh still?

LAURA: Well yea, and now she's had her hours cut even more so... it's a whole thing.

She's really stressed out.

OLLIE: It'll be fine.

LAURA: What?

OLLIE: Her work thing... I'm sure it'll be fine.

LAURA: What does that even mean, what does *'fine'* look like?

OLLIE: Just... over time, odds are... it'll work out.

LAURA: So essentially, it doesn't matter?

OLLIE: I'm not saying that. I'm trying to reassure you that –

LAURA: It's not reassurance, it's nothing. You're deflecting. You're essentially bored of hearing me talk, and you want to conclude it and move on.

OLLIE: Ok, is that genuinely how you feel or have I just touched a nerve?

LAURA: Are you serious?

Silence.

OLLIE: I could not be more lost.

LAURA: What do you mean by *'it'll be fine'*?

OLLIE: I'm trying to make you feel better –

LAURA: Well don't, just, listen.

Silence.

LAURA: What?

OLLIE: I'm listening… oh sorry/ have I somehow fucked that up too?

LAURA: Oh for Christ sake, this actually happens to not be about you.

OLLIE: Then what's it about?

LAURA: It's about the word *'fine'*. Nothing about what I've said looks like it'll be fine, it could get worse, it could stay the same, and yet you've chosen to say *'it'll be fine'*.

OLLIE: Yes, to make you feel –

LAURA: I don't need you to make me feel anything.

OLLIE: See that there, that's about me.

LAURA: Oh my God you're so exhausting/ it actually hurts.

OLLIE: You don't want me to dismiss what you're saying, I get that, and if that's how I made you feel, I am genuinely sorry. But you cannot ban me from saying *'it'll be fine'*.

LAURA: You don't know it'll/ be fine.

OLLIE: And you don't know that it won't.

LAURA: But I don't need to know either way right now. It's not about whether or not she'll be okay in the end – it's about what she's going through *now*. You don't have to solve all my fucking problems. Sometimes it's enough to just listen and say '*That's really shit*' or '*Fuck, that sounds horrible*', or –

OLLIE: Alright. I think what your mum is going through now, must be dreadful. I bet it keeps her up at night. She probably struggles to get out of bed in the morning on the days she actually has work, which aren't as many as they used to be, and God knows what she does on the days she has off. I bet she sits in the car park for a really long time before she builds up the strength to go into work by tapping into that ounce of drive she has left, and when she does, I bet it hurts. But there must be no respite for her when she gets home, because if this is the state of us when we talk about it for five minutes, God knows what it's doing to their marriage.

Silence.

OLLIE: That wasn't…

Look, I'm sorry. I'm sure it'll be…

He stops himself from saying 'fine'.

OLLIE: Okay…

Silence. **LAURA** *is visibly upset.* **OLLIE** *is totally lost.*

OLLIE: Laur?

Come on, I'm sorry. Tell me how she's doing.

Nothing from **LAURA.**

OLLIE: Has she got work tomorrow?

Still nothing.

OLLIE *gets up and heads for the coffee machine. He switches it on. As it's heating up, he goes to speak but retracts. He makes two coffees, and heads back to* **LAURA.** *He places one down for her and sits next to her on the sofa. For a while, they both just sit together in silence.*

OLLIE: Are your socks new?

Silence.

OLLIE: They're nice. Haven't seen you wear socks like that for ages. Don't you think those ones get a bit tight round the top?

LAURA: Do you ever think we have nothing left to talk about?

OLLIE: No, seriously though.

LAURA: I am being serious.

Silence.

OLLIE: You had socks like that when we first met. I thought they were cool. And your trainers. In fact, I reckon I remember your entire outfit from that night. Yea, you had socks like that, white Reebok Classics...

LAURA: I've never owned Reebok Classics.

OLLIE: Well they were that style, like, white, branded trainers.

And a skirt. Or a dress...

LAURA: Jeans.

OLLIE: Jeans. You had a crop top, that wasn't a crop top, but a normal top that you'd made into a crop top. Do you remember?

LAURA: Not really.

OLLIE: I do.

LAURA: I remember the day after.

OLLIE: Ohhh... what did we do?

LAURA: Nothing. Just stayed in.

OLLIE: That's right. *Jurassic World* had just come out and I spent ages finding a stream.

LAURA: That was a shit day.

OLLIE: Uhh I know, fucking appalling remake.

LAURA: No, I mean the day itself, because the night we met you were giving it all that about taking me out the next day.

OLLIE: Was I?

LAURA: Yea, you were gonna take me out for breakfast on Southbank. So full of shit.

OLLIE: I would never say that.

LAURA: You fucking did.

OLLIE: I don't fuck with Southbank, Southbank's dead.

LAURA: Oh my God, you absolutely did. I remember clearly because you said it to get me to stay.

OLLIE: I didn't say that to get you to stay.

LAURA: Then why didn't I leave?

    OLLIE *considers this question.*

OLLIE: Because you were besotted.

LAURA: Fuck off –

OLLIE: The moment you laid eyes on me, you were done. Your goose was cooked.

LAURA: Sometimes you say things, and I throw up in my mouth.

OLLIE: Well don't worry, it wasn't just your goose, my goose was right there too. If anything my goose was in the oven when it was preheating –

LAURA: Can you stop?

OLLIE: I'm not sure I can.

    Silence.

LAURA: I can't believe the year is about to end and I haven't had a night out in months.

OLLIE: You've been working a lot. Besides, next year, we'll make up for it. I say, 2020, we go on a night out every two weeks.

Silence.

Can I say one more thing?

LAURA: Is it about geese?

OLLIE: No, well, not entirely but at one point I may build on the goose analogy, but listen, I didn't think –

OLLIE *moves the coaster on the arm of the sofa, revealing the cigarette burn.* **LAURA** *has nothing, and she knows it.* **OLLIE** *is fixated and doesn't move for what feels like an age.*

LAURA: Before you say anything can I just... Look, I know this is childish... You... we were both saying... Ok, what do you want me –

OLLIE: What I want is for you to use your words, not damage my stuff.

LAURA: Ok, I'll sort it out I promise –

OLLIE: You won't sort anything out. You don't have any consequences to deal with because at the end of the day, you know full well that I can't live with this on my sofa, but it won't bother you, no, you'll be perfectly happy living in squalor. So after a few months of suffering with this, I will go out and buy us a brand new sofa that you will refuse to pay for, because if you did, you would be accepting that you're in the wrong.

LAURA: I am in the wrong.

OLLIE: You are?

LAURA: Yes, 100%.

This is my fault.

OLLIE: This *is* your fault.

LAURA: Yes, it is. And I'm sorry.

OLLIE *has built up rage with nowhere to put it.*

OLLIE: You're sorry. I am glad that you are sorry. I accept your sorry.

LAURA: When I get paid at the end of the month we can go look at getting a new sofa that I will pay for.

OLLIE: I… That might be an overreaction, I mean, you can't really see it.

> **LAURA** *puts a hand on* **OLLIE***'s shoulder, and one on his face, searching for eye contact. Eventually he matches her gaze. She smiles.*

LAURA: How you doing?

OLLIE: I'm cold.

> *Silence.*

OLLIE: I might stick/ the heating on for a bit.

LAURA: You're not putting the heating on.

OLLIE: But I'm cold!

LAURA: Then put on a jumper.

OLLIE: I'm wearing a jumper.

LAURA: Then put another one on.

OLLIE: I'm not putting on two jumpers, I'm not an orphan, I'm in my own home.

LAURA: Go get a blanket.

OLLIE: You go get me one, you're closer to them.

LAURA: No.

OLLIE: Alright I'll stick the heating / on then –

LAURA: Christ fine.

> **LAURA** *heads for the ottoman,* **OLLIE** *braces himself for the balloons. She stops still, looking at a credit card on the floor. She picks it up, still fixed on it.*

LAURA: What's this?

> **LAURA** *holds the card up for* **OLLIE** *to see.*

OLLIE: It's my credit card.

LAURA: Why's it got your dad's name on it?

OLLIE: Well because it's –

It's just a card, a card for emergencies, I barely use it.

LAURA: What kind of emergencies?

OLLIE: Financial emergencies.

LAURA: Financial emergencies?

OLLIE: Yea, it's not a big deal, I've had it since school.

LAURA: You've had it since school?

OLLIE: It gives them peace of mind.

LAURA: What was the last thing you used it for?

OLLIE: Food the other week.

Silence.

LAURA: You used your dad's credit card for my birthday?

OLLIE: No.

Silence.

OLLIE: Not for your presents.

LAURA: You made such a big deal about paying –

OLLIE: I still paid –

LAURA: Your dad paid!

OLLIE: Why can't you just be happy we had a nice time, instead of twisting it into something negative?

LAURA: So, without me knowing it, I'm now indebted to your parents.

OLLIE: You're not indebted to anyone.

LAURA: Right, well be sure to thank your dad from the both of us.

OLLIE: Laur, you have got to stop starting a fight with me over tiny, insignificant things that aren't even a problem. Otherwise, I'd rather not talk. We can just be two grown-ups that cook for each other and have sex.

LAURA: At least then we'd start having sex.

OLLIE: What did you just say?

LAURA: I said at least then we'd start having sex.

OLLIE: We have sex all/ the time –

LAURA: We do not –

OLLIE: Once every three weeks. Unless we're both stressed, or tired but that's normal.

LAURA: It's like you think that as long as you strive for whatever's normal, then you're fine. You couldn't possibly take a step out of your comfort zone.

OLLIE: I like my comfort zone, that's why they call it a *comfort* zone.

LAURA: But maybe every now and again you take a step out of it just to see if you like it, instead of following a set routine like a fucking Bible.

OLLIE: I do not have a routine.

LAURA: Every time we have sex, no matter how long or short or… good, after we stop, you go down on me. And half the time I don't think you even want to.

OLLIE: But you like it?

LAURA: I mean sometimes it's –

OLLIE: You know, only like, thirty percent of guys go down on their girlfriends, so excuse me for being a fucking minority. Besides, when you've been together for as long as we have, you get into a rhythm –

LAURA: Routine.

OLLIE: You figure out what each other like. Next time we can mix it up a bit, we can start with –

LAURA: This. This is what I'm talking about. You don't have to pre-plan everything. There's just no spontaneity and when we're in it, it's like you're not even there, you're so in your head all the time –

OLLIE: Laura, we have sex more times than the average couple, what more do you want?

LAURA: I want you to fuck me. Like, actually, fuck me. I want you... to take control of me. I want you to tie me up and maybe... I don't know... choke me... well not... I want you to let me ride you. Actually ride you until I cum.

Silence.

OLLIE: I'm sorry that I don't find the abuse of women sexy.

LAURA: That is not –

OLLIE: When you really unpack it, the reason that sort of stuff interests you is because of the social conditioning which glorifies rape culture.

LAURA: No when I unpack it I see a guy that's so sexually uncomfortable that he has to use liberal rationale to justify his banal sex drive.

OLLIE: I do not have a banal –

Fine, next time we fuck I'll be sure to slap you about. I'll backhand you. Lots.

I'll let you ride me until you cum even though it makes my legs fall asleep, and when you do cum, I'll buckaroo you off, down the stairs.

And only then if you're unconscious, will I cum all over your face.

Will that make you feel fulfilled in your relationship with me?

Silence.

LAURA: Sounds good.

OLLIE: What?

LAURA: Fuck me. Just like that. Right now.

OLLIE: Fuck you…

LAURA: Right/ now.

OLLIE: Right now.

LAURA: Right now.

   Silence.

LAURA: Ollie.

OLLIE: Yes, okay, away we go.

LAURA: '*Away we go*'?

OLLIE: What?

LAURA: What the do you mean '*away we go*'?

OLLIE: It just means, come on then, let's be having you.

LAURA: Jesus Christ –

OLLIE: It means let's, fuck, now.

LAURA: I love it when you talk dirty to me.

OLLIE: Oh fuck off Laur.

LAURA: Yes.

OLLIE: What?

LAURA: Do that, get angry.

OLLIE: Get…

LAURA: I want you to fuck me, like you want to kill me. Get angry
for me.

OLLIE: I am angry.

LAURA: Tell me.

OLLIE: I'm angry.

LAURA: Yes you are.

OLLIE: I'm really fucking, livid –

LAURA: Livid?

OLLIE: Cross.

LAURA: Cross? Sorry I didn't realise I was fucking a child…

OLLIE: Laura –

LAURA: Maybe this is my fault. Maybe I need to go and find a guy who can actually fuck me like the whore that I am.

OLLIE: Laura, please –

LAURA: Someone who knows –

> **OLLIE** *kisses her to shut her up. They both try to take control of it,* **OLLIE** *comes out on top.* **LAURA** *is happy she's got it out of him. After a beat, he grinds to a halt, which takes them both by surprise.*

LAURA: What's wrong?

OLLIE: Nothing's wrong.

We just –

Just –

> **OLLIE** *continue to kiss her, struggling to undress her. It's all turned quite uncomfortable until they ease to a halt, nothing spectacular.*

> *Silence.*

LAURA: What are you thinking?

OLLIE: I don't know.

LAURA: Tell me.

OLLIE: I'm honestly thinking about nothing.

LAURA: Just… tell me.

OLLIE: I'm thinking… maybe we should go to bed.

LAURA: No, that's not it. What are you *actually* thinking? I can see you're thinking it now, there it is. You're thinking it right now. Whatever that thing is, I can see you telling yourself that you couldn't possibly tell me in a million years. I don't know what it is, but I've seen it's been there for well over a year now, and you think I won't be able to handle it, but I can see it's there so you might as well tell me.

Silence.

OLLIE: Laura –

LAURA: Try me.

Silence.

They both jump as the buzzer for the flat goes off. Neither move.

Silence.

The buzzer goes off again.

Silence.

The buzzer goes off again.

Finally, **LAURA** *exits to the door, leaving* **OLLIE** *alone.*

Silence.

LAURA *re-enters holding a white plastic bag with the top of a brown paper bag visible from inside.*

LAURA: Sorry, when did you order a Chinese?

OLLIE: What?

LAURA: When the fuck did you order a Chinese?

OLLIE *has nothing.*

LAURA: Ollie?

OLLIE: Uhh, I ordered it when you were chatting with your Mum.

LAURA: You ordered it when I was chatting to my Mum.

OLLIE: Yes.

LAURA: So after refusing to eat with my family, and sitting on your phone for three hours while everyone was eating, you've ordered a takeaway for yourself?

OLLIE: No Laur, I ordered it for both of us.

LAURA: I can't even fucking bear…

(Calmly and weighted.) Fuck you.

OLLIE: You're just so ungrateful sometimes, I try and do nice things –

LAURA: I'm ungrateful?

OLLIE: Did you not want a foo yung?

LAURA: No I don't want a foo yung Ol –

OLLIE: Fine! Fuck the foo yung!

> **OLLIE** *snatches the bag from* **LAURA**, *moves to the bin and pops the lid.*

LAURA: What the hell are you doing?

> **OLLIE** *is holding the bag over the bin.*

OLLIE: Well you said you aren't hungry and I'm not gonna eat a whole meal by myself/ I'm not even that hungry myself to be honest –

LAURA: Yea but you don't have to…/ for Christ's sakes don't throw it away.

OLLIE: So wait, you do want the foo yung?

LAURA: Well no, but don't be a monster.

OLLIE: Well say what you like but if you don't want it, it's going in the bin.

LAURA: Don't do that,/ can you even see yourself?

OLLIE: Hey it's you that didn't want it, I'm just doing what/ you want.

LAURA: Oh, you're just doing what I want? Great let's do what Laura wants. Let's take everything and just throw it away, just take all this shit, fuck the takeaway, fuck everything, fuck the bin let's just throw it straight into the ocean, fuck the whales, fuck all of it.

OLLIE: Laura you're being –

LAURA: I'm being what? I'm being irrational? I'm overreacting? I'm triggering you? I'm making you feel small? Being the cause of your depletion in health?

You are a cancer. You're an actual tumour weighing me down, except you're worse. You're worse than fucking cancer – because you've made me fall in love with you, and for four fucking years of my life you have punished me, and twisted me, and made me feel like the worst human being in the world.

You've gotten so fucking good at convincing yourself that you're always the victim. I have never met such a manipulative cunt. How you manage to take all your hate and all your pain, and shove it all onto me, and make me feel like a terrible girlfriend.

You are a sad, broken man. You're not even a man. You're barely a person.

You are a hateful, spiteful, useless shell. And I will never forgive you, because you have made me all of those things now.

Silence.

LAURA: I'm gonna go.

OLLIE doesn't respond. LAURA slowly gets up and picks up her phone, baccy and bag.

She picks up her shoes, considers them, and puts them back down. She moves to get another pair from the ottoman. OLLIE realises too late to stop her. LAURA opens the ottoman.

The balloons float up above her head.

Silence.

LAURA *turns to* **OLLIE**.

Act Two

Late summer, 2015.

Same flat, four and a half years earlier. The lights are off, as streetlight filters in. It's early morning, maybe 3am.

LAURA, *wearing an oversized shirt and a pair of striped white socks on, enters from the bedroom. Unaware of her surroundings and using the light from her phone screen, she searches the flat. Her search leads her off towards the kitchen.*

From the bedroom, a barely conscious **OLLIE** *enters, wearing boxers from the day before. Just as he crosses the room,* **LAURA** *re-enters with a carton of juice.*

OLLIE *screams, which in turn startles* **LAURA**. *It's an unwelcome level of noise for this hour.*

LAURA: Shit!

OLLIE: Fuck! I'm so sorry/ I didn't mean to scare you.

LAURA: I didn't –

OLLIE: I just forgot you were –

LAURA: I was just thirsty –

OLLIE: Do you need a glass?

LAURA: No, well I tried for water, but your tap –

OLLIE: Sometimes it sticks you just have to –

LAURA: I'm good now – juice.

OLLIE: Awesome.

Silence.

LAURA: I couldn't find a glass – I hope that's okay?

OLLIE: Yea sure thing, I mean if you've got anything I've probably contracted it by now anyway.

Silence.

OLLIE: I'll just...

> **OLLIE** *switches on the light, picking up a blanket in a last-second attempt to cover himself.*

> *Silence.*

LAURA: I like your blanket.

OLLIE: Really? Oh, thanks –

It's from Indonesia.

LAURA: Gap year?

OLLIE: Amazon Prime.

> *Silence.*

> **OLLIE** *notices that* **LAURA** *is wearing his shirt.*

OLLIE: Is that my...

LAURA: Oh shit, yea, sorry, I'm wearing your shirt. But not like, in a weird... It's just I needed a / drink, and I didn't know if you had any housemates and I would of grabbed my shirt but it's a crop top and I'm not wearing a –

OLLIE: Oh no, please, it's not weird, I only said it because I couldn't find... honestly, it's fine. You look great, actually, better than I do in it.

LAURA: Thank you.

> *Silence.* **LAURA** *notices that* **OLLIE** *has the blanket around his waist like a sarong.*

LAURA: You alright?

OLLIE: Yea, totally, you?

LAURA: I have seen.../ I'm just saying the mystery is gone, you can chill out a bit.

OLLIE: Seen... oh right yea, I just didn't want to parade my dick around you know?

LAURA: I read it's good for you.

OLLIE: Dick?/ Yea, sleeping naked –

LAURA: Sleeping naked, it's meant to be a lot healthier for you; I do it all the time.

OLLIE: That… that's cool… cool.

Silence.

OLLIE: I'll just…

OLLIE *exits to the bedroom, leaving* **LAURA** *alone. She scans the flat for the first time.*

LAURA: Do you live alone?

OLLIE: *(Off.)* No. Well, technically yes. But there's other flats like this in the same building.

LAURA: Oh, so you like… know the same people on this floor?

OLLIE: *(Off.)* Yea, there's Postman Pat across the way.

OLLIE *enters wearing joggers, pulling a T-shirt over his head. He's holding* **LAURA**'s *jeans.*

LAURA: He's called Pat?

OLLIE: No, I don't know his name, I just…

He gets my post by mistake sometimes. Brings it over.

Silence.

OLLIE: I didn't know if you wanted these or not.

OLLIE *hands her the jeans.*

LAURA: Thanks.

She takes them but doesn't put them on. Instead, she pulls out a pouch of baccy from one of the pockets and starts rolling herself a cigarette.

Silence.

OLLIE: I like your socks.

LAURA: Thanks.

Silence.

LAURA: Sometimes they get a bit tight round the top.

OLLIE: What?

LAURA: Like, round the top.

OLLIE: What do you mean they *get* tight, like, how do socks change tightness?

LAURA: Maybe if they go through a dry spell?

Silence.

OLLIE: Oh, sex.

Silence.

OLLIE: The socks, you meant –

LAURA: Yea.

Silence.

LAURA: Is it alright to smoke out the front?

OLLIE: Yea. I mean… you can just smoke in here. That's what I do.

LAURA: You sure?

OLLIE: Yea, do it all the time.

> **LAURA** *offers* **OLLIE** *the baccy.*

OLLIE: Thanks.

> **LAURA** *lights her cigarette as* **OLLIE** *struggles to roll his.*

OLLIE: Was that your first time in Cargo?

LAURA: No I go all the time/ not sure why though, it's fucking terrible.

OLLIE: Yea, it's such a cool vibe in there… It's so dead, just like, dirty, never good.

LAURA: Yea.

Silence.

OLLIE: That room we met in with all the cheese music, that's not always open is it?

LAURA: We didn't meet in there.

OLLIE: No, you're right... where did we meet exactly?

LAURA: Smoking area.

OLLIE *lights his cigarette.*

OLLIE: Oh Christ, did we smoke a lot because I can feel my throat's just –

LAURA: You didn't, you said you don't smoke.

Silence.

OLLIE: Well... that was a lie.

LAURA: Really?

OLLIE: I smoke... but... not on nights out.

LAURA: Like... the opposite of a social smoker?

OLLIE: Yes.

LAURA: You're an anti-social smoker?

OLLIE: Exactly.

Silence.

OLLIE: We should have got some food on the way back.

LAURA: Should've.

OLLIE: If you want there's a chip shop at the end of the road that's pretty much 24/7.

LAURA: Nah... don't fuck with chip shops in London.

OLLIE: Why?

LAURA: Because they're all terrible. My grandma lives in Devon, the chips they have down there are fucking immense. They've ruined London chips for me.

OLLIE: Surely that's a bit much, I mean, a chip's a chip.

LAURA: I've lived in London my whole life, and in that time I haven't come across one good chip shop.

OLLIE: We don't have to get chips, we could get a Chinese?

LAURA: I sometimes find getting a Chinese is a bit risky, some can be ten-out-of-ten, but some are just grim.

OLLIE: Oh I could murder a Chinese. Crispy duck pancakes. None of that pre-shredded shit. On-the-bone, authentic, English... Chinese cuisine.

LAURA: Are you a racist?

OLLIE: Sorry?

LAURA: I know we're talking about takeaways, it's just your accent –

OLLIE: My accent?

LAURA: And general demeanor. The way you throw the word 'Chinese' around with such... ferocity...

OLLIE: Ferocity?

LAURA: It has a kind of colonialist twang to it.

OLLIE: Sorry?

LAURA: Like it feels dirty in your mouth so you have to wang it out in a certain way.

OLLIE: Are you calling me a colonialist?

LAURA: No, just saying that you have a certain... quality.

OLLIE: Now I feel attacked.

LAURA: Must be weird as a straight white boy being marginalized for the first time.

OLLIE: Sleeping with you doesn't make me a colonialist.

LAURA: Sorry, what/ did you just say?

OLLIE: Oh God, I didn't... that wasn't... I didn't say –

42

LAURA: Do you wanna repeat yourself?

OLLIE: I'm not sure I do.

LAURA: No go on, what is it about fucking me specifically that would/ make you a colonialist?

OLLIE: Well… well you see, because you're… you said/ that you thought –

LAURA: No I know what I said, what did you say?

OLLIE: So, I didn't mean… the joke I meant to say… was… a, a, a, God you know…I mean I didn't mean for you to feel… this is all just like a… the thing/ about colonialism I meant, I didn't mean…

LAURA: Ollie, it's fine, I'm fucking with you.

OLLIE *is caught in his jumper which he's been trying to put on for a while.*

OLLIE: You're fucking with me?

LAURA: Yes.

OLLIE *remains hidden within his jumper.*

LAURA: Do you wanna come out?

OLLIE: Sure.

LAURA *pulls* **OLLIE'S** *jumper over his head. They're the closest to each other they've been.*

Silence.

OLLIE: Sorry, I just… I need to pee.

LAURA: Go pee.

OLLIE *runs off, leaving* **LAURA** *alone again. She pulls out her phone and scrolls.*

After a while, **OLLIE** *re-enters.*

OLLIE: So… I've a feeling I'm not your usual cup of tea.

LAURA: Why'd you think that?

OLLIE: Nothing, I just –

I don't usually do this.

LAURA: No?

OLLIE: Not like, in a bad way.

Well –

I was just in a relationship not long ago.

LAURA: Oh, okay.

OLLIE: But this isn't like a rebound.

LAURA: Didn't say that it –

OLLIE: Shouldn't've said that –

LAURA: I didn't think –

OLLIE: If anything that made it sound like more of a rebound –

LAURA: You talk a lot.

OLLIE: I've been told.

Silence.

OLLIE: Not by her, I wasn't comparing… I don't feel anything towards her anymore.

LAURA: That's probably good then.

OLLIE: *(Abruptly.)* She's a stupid fucking bitch.

LAURA: Right.

Silence.

LAURA: If it's any consolation, I quite like tea.

OLLIE *shoots up and heads towards the kitchen.*

OLLIE: Oh I have chamomile, ginger, ginger with peppermint, ginger without, peppermint without, Earl –

LAURA: You said you're not my usual…

OLLIE: Ah, well I was only joking about the tea –

LAURA: I actually prefer coffee.

OLLIE: My God, me too, I love coffee.

LAURA: Same.

OLLIE: I have one of those mugs… with the thing… *'don't talk to me before I've had'* –

I'll get it and show you.

LAURA: I believe you.

Silence.

OLLIE: The other day I made it to lunchtime without having a cortado, I nearly died.

LAURA: Can I ask you an unrelated question?

OLLIE: Sure.

LAURA: Did you go to private school?

OLLIE: Well, it's a common misconception, they're actually not called private –

LAURA: That's a *solid* yes then?

OLLIE: I did, yea. Is that a problem?

LAURA: Not at all. I have a soft spot for posh boys.

OLLIE: Really? Well, would it interest you to know I've frequented many a yacht in my time?

LAURA: Yea, I bet. Picturing you on a bus is hard.

OLLIE: What's a bus?

LAURA *laughs.*

LAURA: You're not just saying that to get me into bed?

OLLIE: Well, back into bed.

Silence.

OLLIE: Coffee! Would you like a coffee?

LAURA: Do ducks float?

OLLIE: Sorry?

LAURA: Nothing, do you have decaf?

OLLIE: Course.

> **OLLIE** *heads to the coffee machine.* **LAURA** *scans the flat again. She settles on a collection of vinyl records next to a turntable.*

LAURA: So, you collect vinyls.

OLLIE: No?

LAURA: You have loads.

OLLIE: Oh right, them, yea, a lot of them are my dad's old ones. Some are mine. Mainly classics.

LAURA: And classical. You have Debussy…

OLLIE: There's one by Chopin in there.

LAURA: *(Correcting his pronunciation.)* Chopin?

OLLIE: Yea, Chopin, see this…

> *He leans over her and takes a record from the stack she's holding, presenting it to her.*

OLLIE: Lost my virginity to that.

LAURA: You're a loser.

OLLIE: Yea, well you just fucked a loser.

> **OLLIE** *hands* **LAURA** *a coffee.*

LAURA: Well what does that make me?

OLLIE: Pregnant?

> *Silence.*

> **OLLIE** *moves away.*

LAURA: You proud of this?

OLLIE: Yea, that's like a seven-minute symphony and I lasted until the second stanza.

LAURA: It's not a symphony, it's a piano concerto. And there is no second stanza.

OLLIE: How do you –

LAURA: Cellist.

OLLIE: Fuck, really?

LAURA: Grade eight baby.

OLLIE: Well done you.

LAURA: Are you surprised because I'm poor?

OLLIE: No, you just… don't have a cello.

Silence.

OLLIE: When did you start playing the –

LAURA: Are we gonna talk about this all night?

OLLIE: Well, I didn't want to be too personal.

LAURA: I wouldn't worry about being too personal, I can still feel a bit of you dripping down the side of my leg.

OLLIE *recoils.* **LAURA** *backtracks.*

LAURA: Sorry, that/ was a bit…

OLLIE: No, sorry, you're more than welcome to have a shower you know?

LAURA: Nah I'm fine.

OLLIE: I mean, I don't mean I want you to, just if you wanted to. It's not like I need you to wash or…

LAURA: No, honestly it's fine.

OLLIE: I have kitchen roll, that'll do a job?

LAURA: It was a joke.

OLLIE: Oh right. Good one.

Silence.

LAURA: So is it all your mates from Eton/ that need an orchestral accompaniment to ejaculate or are you special?

OLLIE: I didn't go to… alright… what did you lose your virginity to?

LAURA: The sound of the school bins being taken out.

OLLIE: Christ, how old were you?

LAURA: God, well… year eleven I was…

OLLIE: Christ!

LAURA: What?

OLLIE: Well I just –

LAURA: How old were you?

OLLIE: Twelve.

LAURA: Fuck, that's young!

OLLIE: It's not as young as eleven.

LAURA: Yea I guess.

I was sixteen.

OLLIE: When?

LAURA: When I lost my virginity.

OLLIE *stares at her blankly.*

LAURA: I was sixteen when I lost my virginity –

OLLIE: I thought you said… oh right…

Sorry, I wasn't twelve. I was seventeen.

LAURA: What?

OLLIE: I was seventeen when I lost my virginity.

LAURA: But you said you were –

OLLIE: Well I thought you said you were eleven, so I lied, I/ didn't want to seem –

LAURA: Sorry you thought I was eleven when I lost my virginity and you/ didn't find that weird?

OLLIE: Well I didn't want you feeling... I mean everyone has that uncle they hate –

LAURA: What?

OLLIE: Nothing, it was a joke.

Silence.

LAURA: Were you with her long?

OLLIE: Who?

LAURA: Your last girlfriend.

OLLIE: No not that long/ just under two years.

LAURA: Couple of months?/ Two years?

OLLIE: No, just under.

LAURA: Two years is like a lifetime.

OLLIE: Not two years, just under.

LAURA: Just under then.

OLLIE: And it's not a lifetime, you know, unless you're a really sick child.

LAURA: Or, a really healthy child, that gets hit by a bus.

Silence.

OLLIE: Like, I've had a longer relationship with my Nespresso machine, and that doesn't give me half the shit she did –

Silence.

Do you have a lecture tomorrow?

LAURA: Well, tomorrow's Sunday so...

OLLIE: Well, technically it's Sunday morning...

LAURA: Right well in that case, yes, yes I do. Do you?

OLLIE: Nah, Monday off.

LAURA: Where do you go again?

OLLIE: SOAS.

LAURA: *(Surprised.)* Oh right...

OLLIE: I know.

LAURA: Quite a liberal place SOAS?

OLLIE: God yea, you should of seen the day David Cameron got back in... kicked the fuck off.

LAURA: Oh fuck yea, I mean, that was a dark day for everyone, first time I saw my dad actually cry.

OLLIE: Right...

LAURA: I have a feeling I'm going to regret asking this but, who did you vote for?

OLLIE: Well... that depends... who did you vote for?

LAURA: Labour, obviously.

OLLIE: Nice.

LAURA: Come on then, get it over with.

OLLIE: What?

LAURA: Tell me who you voted for.

OLLIE: Labour... Obviously.

LAURA: Who's your local Labour MP?

OLLIE: ... Colin...

LAURA: It's okay to not vote Labour –

OLLIE: I voted Tory.

LAURA: Oh my God, what a plot twist.

OLLIE: Yea.

LAURA: Christ. Should have worn a condom.

OLLIE: I thought this was a safe space?

LAURA: I thought it was too.

Silence.

LAURA: Do you keep that to yourself?

OLLIE: If I admitted that at uni they'd skin me alive.

LAURA: I bet.

Silence.

OLLIE: I just thought Ed Milliband was a bit of a cunt, and my parents have always voted Tory, and I didn't ever think that much about politics.

LAURA: Doubt you needed to.

Silence. **LAURA** *smiles at* **OLLIE,** *he smiles back.* **OLLIE** *awkwardly looks away.* **LAURA** *searches for eye contact.*

OLLIE: I'm really hungry now.

LAURA: Me too.

OLLIE: Would you like me to make you anything?

LAURA: I'm good thanks.

OLLIE: I could make pasta, I have some mushrooms and a little chicken left over, it'd take me minutes to –

LAURA: I'm not actually hungry.

OLLIE: Unless you're vegan? I've got some avocados –

LAURA: Ollie –

OLLIE: I don't know a recipe for them but we could just smash them in a bowl and see what happens?

LAURA: Come kiss me.

OLLIE: Yes.

Silence. **OLLIE** *doesn't move.*

OLLIE: Oh wait, was that a question or a statement?

LAURA: What?

OLLIE: Not a statement, an order.

LAURA: Order?

LAURA *moves to* **OLLIE**.

OLLIE: I don't mean, that makes it sound negative, I don't know how to shut up sometimes it's like this never-ending surge of bullshit. Like, there's tiny men inside me, shoveling away, shouting, '*We need more bullshit in here!*' and it just –

LAURA: Ollie.

Silence.

OLLIE: I could've kissed you then!

LAURA: Then kiss me.

OLLIE: Well I can't, because I ruined the moment.

But don't worry. I will kiss you.

That's a threat.

Just gonna wait for the right moment.

If it comes in the next minute or so, I'll just come get you.

LAURA: Wow.

Silence.

OLLIE: '*Get you*'. Probably the most terrifying thing you can say to someone you've just met. '*I will get you*'.

LAURA: It's like, what are you gonna do when you get me?

OLLIE: You don't know, but I do…

It involves a shovel.

Silence.

OLLIE: See, I will catch you, kill you, beat you, all self-explanatory, but the ambiguity of *'I will get you'* –

LAURA: Is this your first time talking to a girl, like, ever?

OLLIE: No, I mean, I didn't go to school with girls 'til I was seventeen, so I haven't been doing it that long. I'm a better listener though. Go on, say something, and I'll listen, like, really well.

LAURA: Well, for starters, don't just tell me to *'say something'*, start by asking me –

OLLIE: A question, sure… uhh… okay…

What terrifies you the most?

LAURA: Okay… well… my little brother is diabetic. He's only nine, and the fact that it's such a big part of his life already is bad enough, but the whole privatization of the NHS thing is pretty shit, because insulin is so fucking expensive.

OLLIE: Oh God.

LAURA: Yea.

OLLIE: The NHS is going to be privatized?

LAURA *laughs.*

LAURA: It looks very likely, thanks to recent political events.

OLLIE: That's shit… I never –

LAURA: What about you? What terrifies you the most?

OLLIE: Uhh, I think, probably… sharks.

LAURA: No.

OLLIE: What?

LAURA: That's a lie, it's not a real answer.

OLLIE: That's not a lie, sharks are fucking horrendous!

LAURA: No, you said *'terrifies'*, not *'scares'*. They're two completely different things. Tell me what terrifies you.

OLLIE: Sharks terrify me. They're huge. You're in the ocean, a gargantuan environment where you can't move, you can't escape and then this thing, this fucking devil incarnate with a billion teeth –

Shark Week is a fucking joke, if sharks are dying out we should leave that shit to nature.

LAURA: What keeps you up at night? What do you dread? Your parents getting divorced? The crippling unemployment rate for our generation? Losing a loved one?

OLLIE: I don't know, my dad dying, maybe… or my mum. Or both, I'm not sure… what do you want me to say?

LAURA: I don't care what it is, I just want you to be honest, and open and share with me.

OLLIE: I'm trying, really hard, but it's not that easy.

LAURA: You don't need to try, just say what you're thinking. Don't censor.

OLLIE: I'm not censoring –

LAURA: I know you're not censoring but like, there's no right or wrong answer.

OLLIE: Well shark was my answer and you said that was wrong.

LAURA: No, I mean, just say what you're thinking. Look! There it is, I can see you thinking about it right now. Tell me.

OLLIE: Tell you what?

LAURA: That thing, the thought that just went past, there it is again!

OLLIE: What thought?

LAURA: Say it, tell me what you thought about, just then.

OLLIE: I don't… I thought… was thinking… well… when I was younger I was kind of… scared of being alone…

Not that, not being alone but, like… when you never thought school was gonna end, even though all your teachers kept saying it would, but you don't really think about what it's gonna be like, until it happens. And before you even realise it's come to an end, all your mates get into their top choice unis. And even though school was a sack of shit in itself, it's got nothing on how you feel when you're spending everyday at home watching *Doctors* with your mum.

And at that point, that was the worst feeling I'd ever felt.

So because of that feeling… I panicked, and made a rushed application to a uni I didn't really want to go to. And now I'm sat in a crammed lecture hall with people I can't bring myself to get to know, on a course I didn't want to do, all because I thought *that* was lonely.

The ironic thing, the funny thing really, the thing that makes me feel like a complete tit, is that I moved to London to get away from that feeling. Who could ever be lonely in a place where you can get a kebab delivered at four in the morning on a Wednesday?

I was really fucking wrong. Because however bad it felt at Mum and Dad's, London is on a whole other level.

Being in here… on a Friday night… trying to match the different lids to all the Tupperware…

Silence.

LAURA: You've never talked about this before.

OLLIE *shrugs.*

LAURA: You're embarrassed.

OLLIE: Not sure why.

LAURA: Your rock bottom includes you living rent-free at your parents, before moving into a studio flat to go to a uni you applied to on a whim.

OLLIE: And tomorrow, I could decide to fuck it all off, pack everything up, get on a plane and just… go.

I won't do it, but I could.

Who the fuck am I to complain about a single thing?

Silence.

LAURA: Have you ever thought about dropping out?

OLLIE: It's not really an option.

LAURA: Of course it is.

OLLIE: No I mean for my family, not getting into your top choice/ is bad enough, but dropping out of SOAS –

LAURA: How is it any of their…

Wait…

Was your top choice Cambridge?

OLLIE: Christ no. Oxford.

LAURA: Right. Did you really want to go?

OLLIE: Yea, who doesn't want to go to Oxford?

LAURA: Do you really think going there would have made you a better person?

OLLIE: Would have made me a more employable person.

I don't think I would've liked myself. Not that I love myself now, but, I think I'm quite a suggestible person, and… well you know how that hat tells Harry Potter he'd've done well in Slytherin? Well, I think going to Oxford would of made me a cunt.

Neither of them are sure when it happened, but they've found themselves closer than they've been since they woke up.

Silence.

LAURA: Reckon it's bedtime.

OLLIE: Oh. Okay, sure –

OLLIE *breaks away from* **LAURA.**

OLLIE: Do you know where/ all your bits are?

LAURA: Shall we head... Oh, you mean... yea course! I mean the tube's open but...

OLLIE: Oh you don't want to get the tube at this time.

LAURA: You're probably/ right.

OLLIE: An Uber would be safer, surely?

Silence.

LAURA: Yea. Yea, definitely. I'll just grab my...

LAURA *bolts up and starts sweeping the flat for her stuff, dropping bits as she goes.* **OLLIE** *offers to help whilst retracing the last few moments in his head.*

Before he finishes, **LAURA** *is dressed and standing by the door.*

LAURA: So I'm good, thanks/ again for the drink and the... oh no really, it was fun. I've still got your shirt on, sorry.

She goes to take it off.

OLLIE: Honestly, don't thank me, thank you for coming back, sorry, that sounds pathetic I don't mean, thank you for.... the sex was... but getting talk to you... oh no you keep that one, I never wear it, I fucking hate that shirt, but not hate the way it looks, the way... when you wear it, you wearing it now –

Sorry, can I just... I need...

You said, just then... before... that you were gonna head off. Right?

LAURA: Yea.

Silence.

LAURA: I didn't, I didn't say get off, I said '*bedtime*' because apparently I'm a child, but what I meant was should we go back/ to bed, here, yea... no don't apologise it was just a...

OLLIE: Oh Christ, you meant here, I fucking knew it. I just didn't want to assume... I thought you meant you wanted to leave, which you're totally welcome to, I wouldn't want you staying if you didn't feel... but no, I don't want you to go, but I don't want you to feel like you have to stay now just because I've said –

LAURA: What do you want me to do?

OLLIE: Well, I want you to stay.

Silence.

OLLIE: What do you want you to do?

LAURA: That depends.

Let's say I do stay, and not saying that I will, but if I do… hypothetically… what would we do tomorrow?

OLLIE: Well… hypothetically speaking, we could have a lie-in. I have blackout blinds so we could sleep for as long as we want. But we'd probably have to go out at some point because you drank all my juice. So we could go get breakfast somewhere like… Camden? Southbank? Southbank. We'll get breakfast on Southbank and after we could go see a film? Or a play? Or just sit by the Thames? We could talk about how dirty it is. The Thames. I'd tell you some facts, like, how it's actually the cleanest river in the world that runs through a capital city and it's actually a combination of the natural tilt of the riverbed and the mud that causes…

And you'd pull that face, so I'd stop talking about mud. Then we'd… head back here? It would make sense for you to go, but you'd stay. We'd order food and stay up and talk more. Then, eventually we'd sleep. Then we'd wake up and do it all again.

Hypothetically, that's what we could do.

OLLIE *leans in, and kisses* **LAURA.**

They stop for a moment. **LAURA** *leans back in.*

The flat buzzer goes off.

OLLIE: They probably pressed the wrong –

LAURA *kisses* **OLLIE** *again.*

Flat buzzer again.

They ignore it. **LAURA** *leans back onto the sofa, pulling* **OLLIE** *on top of her as they continue to kiss.*

Buzzer a third time. **OLLIE** *breaks away abruptly.*

OLLIE: Don't leave, stay right there / I'm just gonna go murder this person and then we can –

LAURA: Wait, just leave it, it probably doesn't…

OLLIE *goes out, leaving* **LAURA** *on the sofa.*

After a moment, **OLLIE** *re-enters with a takeaway.*

OLLIE: Did you order a Chinese?

LAURA: No?

I mean, yea?

OLLIE: Uhh… sorry, I don't mean to make things weird, but that's a bit…

LAURA: It's just, when we we're talking about it earlier I thought you might –

It was meant to be kinda funny and kinda cute and –

Well after doing it I realised how weird it looked, likc, it was meant to be cool and now it looks like I'm trying to move in, and so, I tried to cancel, they wouldn't process the cancelling –

OLLIE: Mate, I'm fucking with you.

This does make you a bit of a loser.

LAURA: Well, you were just about to fuck a loser.

OLLIE: I was?

LAURA *gives him a look.*

OLLIE: *(Attempting to be assertive.)* I was.

Silence.

OLLIE: You got duck?

LAURA: I did.

They contemplate eating for a moment.

OLLIE: We could/ always eat after

LAURA: Eat after?

OLLIE: Yea.

> **OLLIE** *drops the Chinese as they go for each other.*

> *Blackout.*

www.salamanderstreet.com

Printed in the USA
CPSIA information can be obtained
at www.ICGtesting.com
JSHW012057140824
68134JS00035B/3485

9 781914 228162